W9-DAE-163

000018673 5742
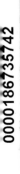

Concordia
Publishing House

Founded in 1869 as the publishing arm of The Lutheran
Church—Missouri Synod, Concordia Publishing House gives
all glory to God for the blessing of 150 years of opportunities
to provide resources that are faithful to the Holy Scriptures
and the Lutheran Confessions.

Published by Concordia Publishing House
3558 S. Jefferson Avenue, St. Louis, MO 63118-3968
1-800-325-3040 · www.cph.org

Text copyright © 2019 Colleen Oakes

All rights reserved. Unless specifically noted, no part of this publication may
be reproduced, stored in a retrieval system, or transmitted, in any form or
by any means, electronic, mechanical, photocopying, recording, or otherwise,
without the prior written permission of Concordia Publishing House.

Manufactured in Shenzhen, China/055760/300702

1 2 3 4 5 6 7 8 9 10      28 27 26 25 24 23 22 21 20 19

# Niko's Night & Day

## A Story of Opposites in God's Creation

Written by Colleen Oakes

Illustrated by Erin Chan

CONCORDIA PUBLISHING HOUSE • SAINT LOUIS

The day had passed,
and night was deep
when Niko
awoke with a start.

"Oh no!" he cried, sitting up in bed. "I left my toy train in the woods!"

No matter how he tried, he couldn't even remember where he left it.

Niko climbed out of bed, feeling nervous. He knew the only way to find his train was to walk the same path he had walked earlier that morning: the path into the woods.

At the door, he pulled a gray wool coat over his striped pajamas and poked his chilly toes into yellow boots. He kissed his cat goodbye and headed out into God's quiet creation.

During the day, the yellow sun had warmed Niko's brown skin.

Now, Niko's heart was beating fast as he entered the woods by his house; they were quiet and still.

Tall trees rose up around him as he walked, their crooked arms casting lines on the ground.

Earlier in the day, he had run his hands over their rough trunks and marveled at the different colors in the bark.

Niko took a breath and counted their trunks as he walked.

1, 2, 3, 4, 5.

This morning, the leafy tree branches overhead had been filled with birdcalls: the bay-bee of the goldfinch, or the thump-thump-thump of the red-bellied woodpecker.

Now, Niko heard only the curious hoot-hoot of a barn owl echo through the trees.

His eyes full of wonder, Niko reached a shallow river.

Earlier in the day, he had watched rainbow trout wriggle hungrily beneath the surface.

Now, the water was black like ink, with only the reflection of the moon overhead. As he watched the water, Niko knew that God could see him here by the river, even in the dark.

As he walked farther, Niko passed a grassy hollow, where earlier he had watched bees working and buzzing back to their hive.

Was his train out here, hidden in the grass?

Sadly, it wasn't, but Niko liked the way he felt as fireflies danced over his head.

He continued on, hoping the train was somewhere out here.
Niko walked through a field, remembering that earlier he
had seen deer grazing among colorful wildflowers.

Now, there were only moonflowers, opening their petals to the sky, and a scruffy raccoon.

"Do you know where my train is?" he asked the raccoon. The raccoon just stared back with a quiet, knowing look.

**Tears** filled Niko's eyes as he passed great-grandfather rock, which during the day had cast its generous shade over him.

Now, the rock was nothing more than a huge shadow with Stars peeking down from behind it. Niko felt small out here, standing by the rock. God, he knew though, was very big.

When Niko reached the farthest fence post in the woods, he let out a sniffle. He hadn't seen his train anywhere, and he was too far from home. It was time to head back.

But then, just as he turned to leave, he noticed a flash of something red with wheels sitting on the fence.

Niko let out a shout of happiness. Could it be? It was!

He had left his train right on the fence rail!

Gently, he cradled it in his arms. "I'm sorry I forgot you!" he whispered.

The red train was wet with dew, but still as good as new.

Niko retraced his steps, and when he got home, he climbed up the stairs and went into his bedroom.

He took off his gray wool coat and bright yellow boots.

He kissed his still-sleeping kitty good night and curled up in his cool bed.

Before he fell asleep, he tucked his *train* safely beside him under the blanket and said a good-night *prayer*.

Then, Niko fell asleep and dreamed of all the wonderful differences between night and day.

And he slept deeply, knowing that the God who loved him was the very same God who had created the sun and the moon, the stars and the rivers, the wildflowers and the animals . . .

and Niko himself.

I hope you enjoyed *Niko's Night and Day*! I penned this book to show a child of God wondering at God's great creation. Each spread contrasts day and night as Niko observes how the world appears during the day and how different, yet similar, it is during the night.

*Niko's Night and Day* simultaneously tells the story of something lost being found. It parallels Jesus' parables of the lost sheep, the lost coin, and the lost son. These parables teach that God is concerned about the lost, anxious that they be returned to Him. They are stories that illustrate the kindness and mercy of our God.

In the parable of the lost sheep, we see God's loving concern for every lost individual and His effort to bring the lost back to Him. The shepherd in this parable is acting as any worthy shepherd would; he seeks out the lost sheep until he finds it, sparing no effort. Here we see an ideal shepherd's love for his sheep and his total commitment to them, just as God proves His love for us by Jesus dying on the cross for our sins.

All of heaven rejoices when the lost are found!

(See Luke 15.)